THE TEN

CW01045673

EASY
GREEK
RECIPES

GREEK COWGIRL

PAN

Pan Macmillan Australia

THIS BOOK HAS BEEN JUDGED BY ITS PEERS AND FOUND TO BE GREEK

First published 1998 in Pan by Pan Macmillan Australia Pty Limited

St Martins Tower, 31 Market Street, Sydney

Copyright © 1998 Billy Blue Merchandising Pty Ltd

Recipes by Helen Tracey and Linda Kaplan

Additional writing by Ross Renwick

Supervising Chefs Matt Blundell and Gavin Cummins

of Kentra Double Bay Australia

Managing Director Aaron Kaplan Creative Director Ross Renwick

National Library of Australia
cataloguing-in-publication data:

Zen, Ziggy
The ten unexpected Greeks just arrived for dinner cookbook;
Easy Greek recipes.

ISBN 0 330 36069 8.

1. cookery, Greek. 1. Title

641.59495

Printed in Australia by McPherson's Printing Group

I HAD BEEN STANDING ON A
ROCK BY THE
AEGEAN SEA
WHEN I WAS
GRABBED BY A
HUGE OCTOPUS.

WITH MY FREE ARM
I OPENED MY GREEK
PHRASEBOOK AND
YELLED THE FIRST SENTENCE
I SAW. LATER I DISCOVERED THAT
I HAD SCREAMED THE WORDS...

'CAN YOU SHOW ME THE WAY TO
THE NEAREST FROCK SHOP?'
IT WORKED. I WAS IMMEDIATELY RESCUED.
SEE RECIPE PAGE 36

HOW TO USE STEALTH AND CUNNING IN THE RUTHLESS GAME KNOWN AS GREEK COOKING

COOKING IS AN AGGRESSIVE SPORT PLAYED BY RUTHLESS HUMANS. BILL CLINTON SAID TO ME THE OTHER DAY THAT A DAY IN THE KITCHEN WAS TOUGHER THAN A DAY WITH HILLARY, ESPECIALLY IF YOU WERE ENTERTAINING.

COOKING FOR YOURSELF IS EASY. IF YOU STUFF IT UP YOU EITHER EAT IT OR EAT OUT.

COOKING FOR OTHERS IS THE ORDINARY PERSON'S EQUIVALENT OF KARAOKE IN FRONT OF ALL THE PEOPLE YOU'RE SCARED OF WHILE NAKED.

SO YOU HAVE TO LEARN TO CHEAT.

HERE'S HOW I CHEATED.

A FEW DAYS AGO, I WAS AT HOME BY MYSELF AT 7 ON A THURSDAY NIGHT AND THE PHONE RANG.

IT WAS BORIS YELTSIN. HE WAS DOWN THE STREET WITH SUGAR PIE deSANTO, BUDDY HOLLY WHO YOU PROBABLY THOUGHT WAS DEAD BUT IT WAS A CIA SCAM, AND ELVIS PRESLEY, SIMILAR STORY.

THEY WERE COMING TO EAT AT MY PLACE, IN HALF AN HOUR.

I RANG THE GREEK TAKEAWAY PLACE AND ORDERED. I PULLED HERBS OUT OF THE NEIGHBOUR'S HERB GARDEN. NO IDEA WHAT THEY WERE CALLED BUT THEY WERE GREEN.

NOW COMES THE IMPORTANT BIT. I HAVE SOME GREAT PROPS.

I got out the brilliant-white tablecloth.
I put the chicken in the big cadmium yellow
bowl. I put the lamb in the bowl that's the
colour of windowsills in Greek islands. The
magenta bowl for the vegetables and the soft
pink bowl for the potatoes. I have an array of
perfectly shaped little bowls of a bright
saffron for the condiments and rather nice
silver candle holders.

I also dragged in a lovely Ionic column from
the neighbour's garden.

I threw the greenery of herbs across
everything and when they walked in a
few moments later they applauded.

All night they talked about Mahler's 4th
Symphony, Guderian's Thrust to the Sea
and flicked through the manuscript of
this little book.

Elvis always surprises me, and he did when
he said that the recipe on page 10, now
called Elvis Michalopoulos's Revenge,
was his favourite dish in the entire world.

I always thought he was a beef and grits man.

Greek café

GREEK MEN SHOUTING
GREEK ROAST LAMB

I used to go to this restaurant in Elizabeth Street across the road from the park. You'd climb up cement stairs, painted classroom green and scuffed, and on the second floor you'd pass a door that was blue.

It was always open and when you looked in thirty swarthy men looked back. Half of them were playing pool and shouting loudly, and the other half were playing cards and shouting loudly. As you passed they smiled at you and shouted loudly.

It was my first introduction to Greek men. From that day I have believed that Greek men hang around in rooms, drink black coffee and retsina, play pool and cards and shout loudly. It may be a racial stereotype but to me it sounds like a perfect life, especially if the room you're shouting in is near a beach.

But this isn't the point of the story. The point of the story is on the next floor where there was a restaurant which was called a lot of zeds on their side and some upside down ns. Where I had my first introduction to Greek roast lamb.

In the restaurant, unlike the room downstairs, there were women as well as men. There was also a lot of shouting.

In ancient Greece lamb was a sacrificial meal and only men were allowed to prepare it.

Although I wasn't there, I'm sure that as they prepared the lamb they shouted.

That's why this lamb recipe has such a silly name.

1 LEG LAMB
2 CLOVES GARLIC, PEELED AND HALVED
1 TABLESPOON SALT
GROUND PEPPER
1 TABLESPOON OREGANO
1 TEASPOON THYME
1 TABLESPOON SPEARMINT FLAKES
JUICE OF 2 LEMONS
3 CUPS BOILING WATER

Put meat in a shallow baking dish.

Use a small knife to make 4 incisions and insert 1 garlic clove half in each.

Rub with salt, pepper, oregano, thyme and spearmint.

Roast at 220° for 30 minutes.

Reduce heat to 150° and bake a further 2 hours.

Add lemon and water for the last half hour and baste lamb well with juices.

Serve with boiled or baked potatoes and a crisp green salad.

ELVIS MICHALOPOULOS'S REVENGE

A TWO-COURSE GREEK MEAL FOR FOUR LASTING FOR SEVERAL DAYS

Buy 12 bottles of retsina (Greek wine).

Put in refrigerator.

Wait one day.

Open first bottle of retsina and drink one glassful.

Put bottle of retsina in brown paper bag and go to shop.

Occasionally drink from brown paper bag parcel. If possible, wear army greatcoat.

Purchase what you need to end up with the following.

BACLAVA

500G FILO PASTRY

250G UNSALTED BUTTER

2 CUPS CHOPPED WALNUTS

POWDERED CINNAMON

1 CUP SUGAR

1 CUP WATER

ANOTHER CUP OF SUGAR

1 CUP HONEY
ANOTHER CUP OF WATER
1 LEMON

You now have the ingredients for Baclava, one of the better-known Greek sweets and better left a few days before consumption.

Return home and in a reflective mood, open another bottle of retsina. It grows on you. Call a friend and open a third bottle of retsina.

When you've got things together a bit, and now being well into your cups, heat 4 ounces of butter together with 1 cup of sugar and 1 cup of water.

Swiftly drink another glass of retsina.

Then add the chopped walnuts.

Line a well-buttered baking dish with 4 sheets of filo, brushing the last one with melted butter mixture.

Spread previous mixture in a thin layer on the pastry. Cover with cinnamon and then spread with two more sheets of buttered filo.

Continue in this manner, interleaving filo and filling until you have run out of either.

Drink another glass of retsina.

Tuck in the ends and sides so stuff doesn't run everywhere, then brush the top with melted butter and score top into diamonds with a knife.

The last layer, by the way, should be about 4 sheets of filo so you won't cut through them during the scoring process.

Bake in a moderate oven until crusty brown.

Take the second cup of sugar, the second cup of water and the juice of 1 lemon and mix it all together.

Boil it and when the previously mentioned golden brown thing comes out of the oven, pour the mixture over the top and leave to cool before cutting into the sort of sizes you see in Greek shops that sell the stuff.

Of course, this whole bloody process can be shortened just by buying the stuff in the first place.

Finish the third bottle of retsina and call three friends inviting them to dinner within a few days. Do not drive and discontinue cooking for the day. Make sure that you have turned the oven off.

Check that there are nine bottles of retsina left.

Do not, on any account, open another.

On the day you have invited your friends, rise early and open one bottle of retsina. Drink one glassful and follow procedures as before.

Tell the man in the shop that you are about to make Kotopoulo Yemisto for four and make sure that you leave with the following ingredients (if he is swarthy, offer him some retsina from your paper bag).

KOTOPOULO YEMISTO
STUFFED CHICKEN

2 SMALL CHICKENS

CHICKEN GIBLETS

1 CUP DRIED WHITE BREAD

1 CUP FINELY CHOPPED ONIONS

1 PAIR OF SWIMMING GOGGLES FROM SPORTS STORE

6 RASHERS OF BACON

OREGANO

SALT

PEPPER

OBVIOUSLY YOU CANNOT BUY BREAD ALREADY DICED AND ONIONS ALREADY FINELY CHOPPED SO GO HOME AND DO IT.

TO DO THE ONIONS PUT ON THE SWIMMING GOGGLES AS THIS WILL STOP YOUR EYES WATERING. HAVING DICED THE BREAD AND CHOPPED THE ONIONS, OPEN FIFTH BOTTLE OF RETSINA AND HANG AROUND UNTIL THE GUESTS ARRIVE, FILLING IN YOUR TIME AS YOU THINK BEST.

WHEN THE DOORBELL RINGS CHECK THAT YOU HAVE TAKEN OFF THE SWIMMING GOGGLES AND OPEN THE DOOR.

ANNOUNCE TO YOUR GUESTS THAT THEY ARE GOING TO HELP YOU COOK KOTOPOULO YEMISTO WITHOUT REVEALING TO THEM THAT THIS ONLY MEANS STUFFED CHICKEN.

TELL THEM ALSO THAT DURING THIS PROCESS THEY WILL BE DRINKING RETSINA AND EATING BACLAVA.

ASSEMBLE THEM IN THE KITCHEN AND OPEN SEVERAL BOTTLES OF RETSINA. AFTER THEY GAG AND HEAVE ABOUT A BIT, TELL THEM THAT RETSINA IS AN ACQUIRED TASTE AND THAT THEY ARE ABOUT TO ACQUIRE IT. TOAST LUCULLUS, THE FIFTH-CENTURY FATHER OF GREEK COOKING, AND BEGIN TO LOOK REASONABLY HELPLESS. SOMEONE WILL ALWAYS TAKE CHARGE AND KEEP THE COOKING GOING. YOUR ONLY RESPONSIBILITY NOW IS TO KEEP THE RETSINA FLOWING AND TO MAKE SURE THAT YOUR GUESTS FOLLOW THE FOLLOWING INSTRUCTIONS.

WASH THE CHICKENS AND PREPARE THE STUFFING.

CHOP UP GIBLETS WITH 3 RASHERS OF BACON AND MIX TOGETHER WITH THE FINELY CHOPPED ONION AND THE DICED BREAD.

ADD SALT, PEPPER AND A PUFF OF OREGANO.

STUFF THE BIRDS WITH MIXTURE. BUTTER BIRDS ON THE OUTSIDE AND ROAST IN OVEN.

ABOUT 15 MINUTES BEFORE REMOVING THE BIRDS FROM THE OVEN, HAVE THE PERSON WHO HAS DRUNK THE LEAST RETSINA COVER THE BREASTS WITH THE REMAINING PIECES OF BACON.

BEFORE SERVING, DISCOVER YOU HAVE FORGOTTEN TO SET THE TABLE AND HAVE SOMEONE DO IT FOR YOU.

SERVE MEAL AND OPEN REMAINING BOTTLES OF RETSINA. FEEL RESPONSIBLE FOR THE SECOND DUTY BUT NOT THE FIRST.

BEEF OR LAMB SOUVLAKI

CUT MEAT INTO $2^1/_2$ CM CUBES.

PLACE 4-5 PIECES ON SKEWERS.

SPRINKLE WITH OLIVE OIL, LEMON JUICE, GARLIC,
SALT AND OREGANO.

GRILL FOR 5 MINUTES, TURNING ONCE.

FILLET OF HAM LOUTSA

A RECIPE FROM CYPRUS

PREHEAT OVEN TO 200°.

RUB A BONED, SCORED PORK LOIN WITH GARLIC, SALT,
BLACK PEPPER, LEMON JUICE, CORIANDER AND CUMIN.

BAKE FOR 20 MINUTES THEN REDUCE TO 175° FOR
APPROXIMATELY 3 HOURS OR UNTIL COOKED.

SLICE FINELY. CAN BE SERVED HOT OR COLD.

UNEXPECTED BIKINI

COS SOUP
GREEK VEGETABLE SOUP

500G MEATY SOUP BONES
2 LITRES COLD WATER
2 TEASPOONS SALT
3 MEDIUM CARROTS, CHOPPED
4 CELERY STALKS, WITH LEAVES, CHOPPED
2 MEDIUM ONIONS, CHOPPED
2 MEDIUM POTATOES, CUBED
2 FRESH TOMATOES, DICED
1 BAY LEAF
1 TABLESPOON PLAIN FLOUR

BRING TO BOIL BONES, WATER AND SALT FOR 1 HOUR.

SKIM OFF SCUM WHICH FLOATS TO THE TOP.

STRAIN BROTH AND RETURN TO POT.

ADD ALL VEGETABLES AND THEN SIMMER FOR 1 HOUR.

MAKE SMOOTH PASTE WITH FLOUR AND 1/2 CUP COLD WATER.

SLOWLY ADD TO BROTH, WHISKING TO THICKEN.

GREEK DOG SURPRISED
BY UNEXPECTED BIKINI

ALI PASHA PILAF

TOMATO PILAF

SERVES 8.

2 TABLESPOONS EACH OF BUTTER AND OLIVE OIL

2 MEDIUM ONIONS, CHOPPED

1 CLOVE GARLIC, MINCED

$1/2$ GREEN CAPSICUM, CUT INTO THIN STRIPS

1 400G CAN TOMATOES

3 CUPS CHICKEN BROTH

$1/2$ CUP WHITE WINE

1 LARGE PINCH OF SAFFRON

PEPPER AND 2 TEASPOONS SALT

1 TEASPOON SUGAR

500G RAW OR COOKED MEAT (CHICKEN, BEEF, VEAL, PORK)

2 CUPS LONG-GRAIN RICE

2 CUPS MIXED SEAFOOD, RAW OR COOKED PRAWNS, CRAB, CLAMS, MUSSELS, OCTOPUS, SQUID, PIPIS, SCALLOPS

PARSLEY AND LEMON WEDGES FOR GARNISH

HEAT BUTTER AND OIL IN A LARGE FRYPAN.

FRY ONION, GARLIC AND CAPSICUM FOR 5 MINUTES ON A MEDIUM HEAT.

IF USING RAW MEAT, ADD AT THIS TIME.

FRY A FURTHER 10 MINUTES, THEN ADD TOMATOES, BROTH, WINE AND SEASONINGS.

BRING TO THE BOIL, ADD RICE.

STIR OCCASIONALLY AND COVER.

REDUCE HEAT AND SIMMER FOR 20 MINUTES, STIRRING A COUPLE OF TIMES TO AVOID STICKING.

ADD SEAFOOD AND COOKED MEATS AND COOK FOR A FURTHER 10 MINUTES.

SERVE HOT WITH CHOPPED PARSLEY AND LEMON WEDGES AND WITH A SIDE SALAD.

THE FLASH GREEK
ELVIS MICHALOPOULOS
WHO WAS LITTLE HELP
WITH THIS BOOK,
BUT HELPED WITH
THE HEAVY DRINKING

GREEK SALADS

CUCUMBER SALAD WITH YOGHURT

**2 CUCUMBERS, PEELED, SEEDED
AND THINLY SLICED**

DRESSING:

**1 CUP YOGHURT
1 TEASPOON VINEGAR
1 TEASPOON FRESH MINT
1 TEASPOON CHOPPED SHALLOTS
1/2 TEASPOON SUGAR
SALT AND PEPPER**

MIX CUCUMBERS AND DRESSING AND SERVE CHILLED.

POSEIDON, GOD OF COWGIRLS

TOMATO SALAD SANTORINI

8 RIPE, MEDIUM TOMATOES
1/2 MEDIUM ONION, CHOPPED
1 CUCUMBER, THINLY SLICED
SALT AND PEPPER
1 TEASPOON FRESH OREGANO
**   OR MARJORAM**
1/4 CUP OLIVE OIL

ADD ALL INGREDIENTS AND TOSS LIGHTLY.

SERVE AT ROOM TEMPERATURE.

IF SERVING AS A SALAD, SERVE WITH SLICES
OF BREAD FOR DIPPING.

GREEK COWGIRLS ARE FAMOUS
FOR THEIR TOMATO SALADS
AND THEIR STRANGE HATS

CARROTS AND HONEY

CENTURIES AGO, DIPHLIUS, A GREEK PHYSICIAN, WARNED THAT EATING CARROTS AROUSES SEXUAL DESIRE. THE GREEKS KEEP ADDING CARROTS TO THEIR FAVOURITE RECIPES. THIS DISH IS A GREEK FAVOURITE.

1KG MEDIUM CARROTS, PEELED AND SLICED

WATER TO COVER

1 PINCH NUTMEG

1/2 CUP HONEY

1/4 CUP BUTTER

SALT AND PEPPER

1 TEASPOON MINT

COVER CARROTS WITH WATER AND BRING TO THE BOIL.

COVER AND SIMMER FOR 20 MINUTES, OR UNTIL SOFT.

MELT THE BUTTER AND ADD THE HONEY UNTIL BUBBLING.

DRAIN CARROTS AND ADD THEM, NUTMEG AND THE MINT TO THE SYRUP.

SEASON.

EGGPLANT BYZANTINE

1 LARGE EGGPLANT, CUT INTO 1 CM SLICES

1 CUP FLOUR

1/4 CUP GRATED CHEESE

2 BEATEN EGGS

1 CUP OIL FOR FRYING

SALT

SAUCE:

TOMATO SAUCE (GREEK TOMATO SAUCE, PAGE 57)

WASH AND SLICE EGGPLANT.

SPRINKLE WITH SALT AND STAND FOR 30 MINUTES.

RINSE WELL, PAT DRY.

DIP IN THE COMBINATION OF FLOUR AND CHEESE, COATING WELL, THEN DIP IN EGG.

REPEAT THIS STEP.

FRY IN HOT OIL UNTIL BROWN ON BOTH SIDES – AROUND 10 MINUTES.

SERVE WITH THE TOMATO SAUCE.

STUFFED EGGPLANT

EPIMENIDOU LANE

ALLOW 1/2 MEDIUM EGGPLANT PER PERSON.

FILLING:

2 TABLESPOONS OIL

500G GROUND BEEF OR LAMB

2 MEDIUM ONIONS, FINELY CHOPPED

1 CLOVE GARLIC, MINCED

2 CUPS WATER

1/2 CUP TOMATO SAUCE

1 CUP SHORT-GRAIN RICE

1 TEASPOON EACH OF FRESH MINT AND PARSLEY

1/2 TEASPOON SALT

PEPPER

1/2 CUP CURRANTS OR SULTANAS

1/8 TEASPOON CINNAMON

1/4 CUP PORT WINE

1/4 CUP PINE NUTS

2 CUPS WATER

JUICE OF 1 LEMON

TOPPING:

1 CUP BREADCRUMBS
1/2 CUP GRATED CHEESE

CUT OFF TOPS OF EGGPLANTS.

CUT IN HALF AND SCOOP OUT FLESH WITH SMALL PARING KNIFE, BEING CAREFUL NOT TO PIERCE THE SKIN.

CHOP PULP AND ADD TO PARTIALLY COOKED AND PREPARED FILLING.

FILL THE HALVES AND SPRINKLE WITH COMBINED BREADCRUMBS AND CHEESE.

PLACE HALVES SIDE BY SIDE IN A BAKING DISH.

ADD 2 CUPS WATER AND BAKE FOR 45 MINUTES ON MEDIUM HEAT.

SYMI

MOUSSAKA

1 LARGE EGGPLANT
SALT
$\frac{1}{2}$ CUP OIL
115G MARGARINE OR BUTTER

WHITE SAUCE:

2 CUPS MILK
2 TABLESPOONS CORNFLOUR
$\frac{1}{2}$ TEASPOON SALT
4 EGGS, LIGHTLY BEATEN

FILLING:

500G GROUND LAMB OR BEEF
2 MEDIUM ONIONS, CHOPPED
1 CLOVE GARLIC, MINCED
$\frac{1}{2}$ CUP CHOPPED PARSLEY
$\frac{1}{2}$ CUP HOME-COOKED TOMATO SAUCE
$\frac{1}{2}$ CUP WHITE WINE
1 CUP WATER
2 TABLESPOONS BUTTER
4 TABLESPOONS OLIVE OIL

TOPPING:

1 CUP GRATED CHEESE
1/4 TEASPOON CINNAMON OR NUTMEG

SLICE EGGPLANT INTO 1CM SLICES, SALT AND STAND FOR 30 MINUTES. RINSE WELL, THEN PAT DRY.

PLACE SLICES SIDE BY SIDE ON AN OILED BAKING TRAY.

MELT BUTTER AND OIL AND BRUSH TOPS LIGHTLY.

BAKE IN A PREHEATED MODERATE OVEN 180° FOR 10 MINUTES. REMOVE FROM OVEN.

FILLING:

HEAT 1 TABLESPOON OF BUTTER AND 2 TABLESPOONS OF OIL, MIX IN A FRYING PAN AND FRY ONIONS UNTIL TRANSPARENT.

ADD MEAT AND REMAINING INGREDIENTS.

COOK FOR 10 MINUTES.

PLACE A LAYER OF EGGPLANT IN A CASSEROLE DISH AND SPREAD WITH MEAT FILLING.

ADD REMAINING EGGPLANT ON TOP. BRUSH WITH REMAINING BUTTER AND OIL MIX.

PREPARE WHITE SAUCE.

ADD EGGS AND POUR OVER THE TOP OF THE EGGPLANT.

SPRINKLE WITH CHEESE, CINNAMON AND ANY REMAINING BUTTER AND OIL.

BAKE IN MODERATE OVEN FOR 45 MINUTES.

TO SERVE, CUT IN SQUARES.

ANTONIO'S OKRA

OKRA WITH TOMATOES

2 CLOVES GARLIC, CRUSHED

500G FRESH OKRA

1 TABLESPOON OIL

1 CUP CHOPPED ONION OR LEEKS

1 CUP CHOPPED TOMATOES

1 TABLESPOON CHOPPED PARSLEY

1 CUP WATER

JUICE OF 1 LEMON

1 BAY LEAF

SALT AND PEPPER

1 TABLESPOON VINEGAR

CUT STEMS OFF OKRA, BEING CAREFUL NOT TO
EXPOSE THE SEEDS.

COVER WITH WATER, 1 TEASPOON OF VINEGAR AND SALT
AND LET STAND FOR 15 MINUTES.

DRAIN, RINSE AND DRY. HEAT THE OIL, ADD THE ONIONS
AND GARLIC AND FRY FOR 5 MINUTES.

ADD THE REMAINING INGREDIENTS AND COVER, REDUCING
THE HEAT TO MEDIUM.

COOK FOR 25 MINUTES UNTIL TENDER AND SERVE
SPRINKLED WITH CHOPPED PARSLEY AND CRUSTY BREAD.

TAVERNA POTATO SALAD

8 POTATOES, UNPEELED
2 LITRES WATER
1 TEASPOON SALT
1 MEDIUM ONION, FINELY CHOPPED

DRESSING:

$1/2$ CUP OLIVE OIL
JUICE OF 2 LEMONS
$1/2$ TEASPOON SALT
PEPPER
2 TEASPOONS OREGANO AND/OR PARSLEY
$1/2$ TEASPOON SUGAR

BOIL WHOLE POTATOES IN SALTED WATER UNTIL TENDER —
FOR ABOUT 45 MINUTES.

MIX THE DRESSING WHILE POTATOES ARE BOILING.

ADD THE ONIONS TO THE DRESSING AND ALLOW
TO STAND FOR 30 MINUTES.

PEEL POTATOES WHILE HOT, CUT INTO CUBES.

POUR MIXTURE OVER HOT POTATOES AND TOSS WELL.
SERVE WHILE STILL WARM.

THE SECRET OF THIS RECIPE IS TO MARINATE THE
ONIONS IN THE DRESSING BEFORE MIXING THEM
INTO THE HOT POTATOES.

MYKONOS MOON FISH

BAKED FISH

WHOLE FISH (SNAPPER OR BREAM), 1.5KG

MARINADE:

$1/2$ CUP OLIVE OIL

SALT

JUICE OF 1 LEMON

GROUND PEPPER

$1/2$ CUP WHITE WINE

$1/2$ TEASPOON TARRAGON, THYME,
   ROSEMARY, PARSLEY

BLACK OLIVES AND FETA CHEESE
   FOR GARNISH

PLACE RINSED FISH IN BAKING DISH.

POUR MARINADE OVER FISH AND PUT IN FRIDGE FOR
AT LEAST $1/2$ HOUR.

TURN FISH DURING MARINATING, MAKING SURE ALL
THE FISH IS BASTED.

POUR OFF SOME OF MARINADE INTO A JUG.

BAKE IN MODERATE OVEN 180° FOR 1 HOUR COVERED.
REMOVE COVER AFTER 35 MINUTES AND BASTE
FREQUENTLY WITH SAVED MARINADE UNTIL TENDER.

SERVE WHOLE, GARNISHED WITH BLACK OLIVES, FETA
CHEESE AND/OR RAW VEGETABLES.

MYKONOS GREEK/TURKISH COFFEE

SERVES 4.

4 DEMITASSE CUPS WATER
4 TEASPOONS SUGAR
4 HEAPED TEASPOONS EUROPEAN COFFEE

IN A SMALL POT, BRING WATER AND SUGAR TO THE BOIL.
REMOVE FROM THE HEAT AND STIR IN COFFEE.

RETURN TO THE HEAT – COFFEE WILL BOIL TO THE TOP
IMMEDIATELY, SO BE READY TO REMOVE FROM THE HEAT.

PUT POT ON THE HEAT A SECOND TIME AND WAIT UNTIL
IT BOILS TO THE TOP AGAIN.

TAKE OFF, AND REPEAT FOR A THIRD TIME.

POUR IMMEDIATELY INTO A DEMITASSE CUP,
FILLING IT $3/4$ FULL.

ELVIS THE FLASH GREEK FISH
ALSO KNOWN AS BAKED FISH FILLETS

FIRST THING I'D DO IS GRAB ABOUT A KILO OF BONELESS WHITE FISH. AND A NICE BONELESS CHARDONNAY TO TAKE SHOPPING WITH YOU. DRINK FROM THE BOTTLE IF YOU WISH. DON'T BLAME ME. PEOPLE ARE GETTING MORE AND MORE NARROW-MINDED.

DO A 1/4 OF A CUP OF OLIVE OIL, 4 THINLY SLICED ONIONS, 2 CLOVES OF CRUSHED GARLIC, 2 CUPS OF CHOPPED TOMATOES AND 1 CUP OF TOMATO PUREE.

THIS RECIPE WAS ONCE A BARBECUE. NOW IT'S A BAKE.

IF YOU'RE RUNNING OUT OF CUPS HAVE ANOTHER CUP OF CHARDONNAY AND RINSE THE CUP. PUT IN IT **1/2 A CUP OF CHOPPED PARSLEY.** KEEP SEARCHING FOR CUPS AND DRINK FROM THE BOTTLE.

NOT LONG AGO, I THOUGHT THAT I NEEDED A BARBECUE. I WENT TO THE USUAL PLACES.

I ONLY WANTED TO COOK A CHOP. I WASN'T ENTERTAINING AT VERSAILLES. JUST A CHOP.

THE LEAST UGLY BARBECUE COULD FIT ABOUT SEVENTY CHOPS AND HALF A DEER.

THERE WERE UGLY LITTLE SIDE BITS WHERE YOU COULD GUT FISH OR WILDEBEEST.

THERE WAS A SILVER BOTTLE FULL OF GAS. IF YOU MAKE

A MISTAKE WITH THIS SORT OF GAS MOST OF YOUR
NEIGHBOURS ARE AT GROUND ZERO AND PEOPLE FIVE
BLOCKS AWAY WILL BE INJURED BY FLYING CHOPS.

IT WAS EXPENSIVE. IT WAS UGLY. IT WAS DANGEROUS.
I BOUGHT IT.

I COOKED MY CHOP. I PUSHED THE BARBECUE OUT OF
SIGHT AND NEVER USED IT AGAIN.

IT THEN REVEALED ITS FINEST QUALITY.
IT RUSTED QUICKLY.

THE SUN ALL DAY AND THE MOON AT NIGHT AND YOU
CAN'T BUY A GOOD-LOOKING BARBECUE FOR LOVE OR
MONEY. AND DON'T START ME ON OUTDOOR FURNITURE.

ANYWAY, YOU WON'T NEED A BARBECUE FOR THIS DISH.

YOU WILL NEED **1 TEASPOON OF OREGANO, A 1/4 TEASPOON OF CINNAMON, SALT, PEPPER AND 1/2 A CUP OF WHITE WINE.**

OIL BAKING PAN WITH HALF THE OLIVE OIL.
PLACE RINSED FISH IN PAN.

SAUCE:

FRY ONIONS AND GARLIC IN REMAINING OIL UNTIL
TRANSLUCENT (ABOUT 5 MINUTES). ADD REMAINING
INGREDIENTS, COVER AND COOK FOR 10 MINUTES.

POUR SAUCE OVER FISH AND BAKE IN MODERATE OVEN
180°, FOR 30 MINUTES OR UNTIL TENDER.

SERVE WITH CRUSTY BREAD AND A CRISP SALAD.

TRIPODOU STREET

TARAMASALATA

1 100G JAR TARAMA
2 CUPS FRESH BREADCRUMBS
½ PACKET LIGHT PHILADELPHIA CHEESE
1 SMALL CLOVE OF GARLIC, CRUSHED
JUICE OF 1-2 LEMONS
1 CUP OLIVE OIL
½ ONION, FINELY CHOPPED

BLEND ALL INGREDIENTS IN BLENDER.

CHILL.

USE AS DIP OR SPREAD, SERVED WITH PLAIN BISCUITS
(WATER CRACKERS) AND RAW VEGETABLES.

ALSO SERVE A BOWL OF BLACK OLIVES.

ANVIL I BOUGHT IN TRIPODOU STREET
AS A GIFT FOR BORIS YELTSIN

ERMOU STREET

FISH MARINADE

1 CUP WHITE VINEGAR

1 CLOVE GARLIC, CRUSHED

1/2 CUP OLIVE OIL

JUICE OF 1 LEMON

1/2 TEASPOON EACH OF THYME, MARJORAM, TARRAGON, OREGANO OR PARSLEY

1/2 CUP WHITE WINE

MARINATE FISH PRIOR TO BAKING, GRILLING, FRYING OR BARBECUING.

THIS CAN BE USED AS A BASTE.

IT IS ALSO IDEAL OVER SKEWERED FISH.

PLACE CHUNKS OF BONELESS FISH ON SKEWERS.

SQUID, PRAWNS AND OCTOPUS CAN ALSO BE USED.

DIP IN MARINADE (OR EVEN BETTER, MARINATE FOR A FEW HOURS). GRILL OR PLACE ON BARBECUE.

Underpants I bought in Ermou Street
as a gift for Prince Philip

HEARTBREAK HOTEL OCTOPUS
OCTOPUS IN RED WINE

1KG FRESH BABY OCTOPUS

40ML OLIVE OIL

1 CLOVE GARLIC, CRUSHED

1 MEDIUM ONION, QUARTERED

1 BAY LEAF

200ML DRY RED WINE

30ML RED WINE VINEGAR

200ML TOMATO PUREE

1 CHICKEN STOCK CUBE

1 TEASPOON DRIED OREGANO

1 TEASPOON SUGAR

SALT AND PEPPER

2 TABLESPOONS CHOPPED PARSLEY

REMOVE HEAD FROM OCTOPUS.

REMOVE BEAK AND QUARTER.

HEAT OIL. ADD ONION AND GARLIC AND FRY
UNTIL GARLIC IS A LIGHT GOLDEN COLOUR.

ADD OCTOPUS, STIRRING OVER MODERATE
HEAT FOR 5 MINUTES.

ADD REMAINING INGREDIENTS EXCEPT PARSLEY.

SIMMER FOR 1 HOUR OR UNTIL TENDER.

REMOVE BAY LEAF, CORRECT SEASONING.

SPRINKLE WITH CHOPPED PARSLEY BEFORE SERVING.

PLAKA
STUFFED SQUID

ALLOW 3 SQUID PER PERSON

STUFFING:
1 CUP RICE

SALT

CAYENNE PEPPER

1 CUP TOMATO JUICE

1 CLOVE GARLIC, CRUSHED

1/4 CUP CURRANTS

1/4 CUP PINE NUTS

1/2 CUP WATER

1/4 CUP OLIVE OIL

JUICE OF 1 LEMON

CLEAN AND RINSE SQUID SACS. COOK RICE IN OTHER INGREDIENTS FOR 30 MINUTES. COOL A LITTLE.

FILL SACS WITH STUFFING. SPREAD LEFTOVER RICE IN A BAKING DISH AND PLACE SQUIDS ON TOP. BRUSH WITH OIL AND BAKE ON MEDIUM HEAT FOR 10 MINUTES.

PIRAEUS PRAWNS
PRAWN CASSEROLE

500G GREEN PRAWNS

1 CUP WHITE WINE (250ML)

2 TABLESPOONS OLIVE OIL

3 TOMATOES, CHOPPED

1 MEDIUM ONION, CHOPPED

1 CLOVE GARLIC, CRUSHED

PINCH OF SUGAR

SALT AND PEPPER

1 TABLESPOON BRANDY

250G FETA CHEESE

1 TEASPOON OREGANO OR PARSLEY

SHELL AND DEVEIN PRAWNS (TO DEVEIN, MAKE A SMALL INCISION DOWN LENGTH OF PRAWN'S BACK. THEN LIFT OFF THE BLACK VEIN).

BOIL PRAWNS IN WHITE WINE FOR 1 MINUTE, UNTIL LIGHT PINK COLOUR.

HEAT OIL IN FRYPAN AND FRY PRAWNS OVER MEDIUM HEAT FOR 3 MINUTES UNTIL FULLY PINK.

RETAIN OIL.

PUT PRAWNS IN SERVING DISH.

ADD ONION, TOMATOES AND GARLIC TO FRYPAN
AND COOK FOR 5 MINUTES.

ADD ALL OTHER INGREDIENTS EXCEPT FETA CHEESE.

POUR OVER PRAWNS AND ADD CRUMBLED FETA.

SERVE IMMEDIATELY.

PRAWNS HANG AROUND IN SCHOOLS.
THIS IS NOT A SCHOOL,
IN FACT IT'S NOT EVEN A PRAWN

OMONIA SQUARE CHICKEN

BAKED CHICKEN WITH LEMON
AND OREGANO

1 1.4KG CHICKEN

200G BUTTER

1/4 CUP OLIVE OIL

2 TEASPOONS SALT

GROUND PEPPER

**1 TABLESPOON EACH OF OREGANO
   AND PARSLEY**

JUICE OF 2 LEMONS

3 CUPS BOILING WATER

2 TABLESPOONS FLOUR

HEAT BUTTER AND OIL.

POUR HALF INTO A BAKING DISH AND ADD WHOLE CHICKEN.

SPRINKLE WITH OREGANO, PARSLEY, SALT AND PEPPER.

MIX LEMON JUICE WITH REMAINING OIL/BUTTER MIXTURE.

USE FOR BASTING.

BAKE AT 200° FOR 20 MINUTES THEN 180° FOR $1^1/_2$ HOURS.

BASTE SEVERAL TIMES DURING ROASTING.

PUT CHICKEN ON SERVING PLATTER.

RETAIN JUICES IN PAN FOR GRAVY.

LEMON CHICKEN GRAVY:

ADD BOILING WATER TO PAN.

SCRAPE THE BOTTOM AND MIX IT IN.

MIX FLOUR IN $^1/_2$ CUP COLD WATER AND STIR INTO PAN.

SERVE WITH GREEN VEGETABLES, RICE OR BOILED POTATOES.

TO BE A GREAT GREEK COOK
IT'S BEST TO HAVE YOUR
OWN OLIVE GROVE

SANTORINI BICYCLE CLUB CHICKEN
CHICKEN TAVERNA WITH TOMATOES

1 1.4KG CHICKEN

200G BUTTER

2 TABLESPOONS OLIVE OIL

JUICE OF 1 LEMON

SALT AND PEPPER

2 400G CANS TOMATOES

1 5CM CINNAMON STICK

1 MEDIUM ONION, THINLY SLICED

1 TABLESPOON OREGANO

1 TEASPOON MARJORAM

1 BAY LEAF

1/2 CUP RED WINE

PINCH OF SUGAR

HEAT BUTTER AND OIL.

POUR HALF INTO A BAKING DISH AND ADD WHOLE CHICKEN.

SPRINKLE WITH OREGANO, SALT AND PEPPER.

MIX LEMON JUICE WITH REMAINING OIL/BUTTER MIXTURE.

USE FOR BASTING.

SPRINKLE WITH SALT AND PEPPER AND BAKE AT 200° FOR 30 MINUTES.

PUT REMAINING INGREDIENTS IN POT, BRING TO THE BOIL AND POUR OVER CHICKEN.

REDUCE OVEN TO 170°-180°. BAKE FOR
1-1¹/₂ HOURS MORE.

SERVE OVER A BED OF RICE OR PASTA WITH A CRISP SALAD.

THE BICYCLE DRAWING
DIDN'T TURN OUT TOO WELL
SO I'VE SUBSTITUTED
A MAN PUSHING A BEAR

MIRABELLO

SOUVLAKIA

**250G MEAT PER PERSON —
BEEF, LAMB, KIDNEYS, LIVER**

2 FIRM TOMATOES, CUT IN QUARTERS

**TINY WHOLE ONIONS, OR
1 ONION, QUARTERED**

1 GREEN CAPSICUM, CUT IN SQUARES

8 MUSHROOMS, SEPARATE STEMS AND CAPS

SALT AND PEPPER

OREGANO AND PARSLEY

JUICE OF 1 LEMON

CUBE MEAT. PREPARE VEGETABLES.

SKEWER IN FOLLOWING ORDER: CAPSICUM, MUSHROOM
STEM, ONION, MEAT, TOMATO, AND CONTINUE UNTIL
$3/4$ FULL. TOP OFF WITH MUSHROOM CAP.

PLACE SKEWERS IN SHALLOW BAKING DISH.

SPRINKLE WITH REMAINING INGREDIENTS AND GRILL, ABOUT
5 MINUTES ON EACH SIDE.

OVERCOOKING WILL DRY THEM OUT! SERVE IMMEDIATELY –
CAN BE AN APPETISER, OR A MEAL, SERVED ON A BED OF RICE.

THE LAMB YOU CAN GET ON THE OTHER ISLAND

LAMB AND LEEKS

2 TABLESPOONS OIL
1KG LEG OF LAMB, CUT IN CUBES
1 CLOVE GARLIC, PEELED AND HALVED
1 BUNCH LEEKS, CUT IN PIECES
1 MEDIUM CARROT, SLICED
2 TEASPOONS SALT
GROUND PEPPER
3 CUPS WATER

HEAT OIL AND BROWN LAMB ON HIGH FOR 10 MINUTES, STIRRING CONTINUALLY. ADD REMAINING INGREDIENTS, COVER AND REDUCE HEAT.

SIMMER FOR 2 HOURS. SERVE WITH CRUSTY BREAD AND RETSINA.

MARINATED MUSHROOMS

WIPE MUSHROOMS WITH DAMP CLOTH AND SIMMER IN 2 TABLESPOONS SALTED WATER 4 MINUTES.

COOL AND ADD $1/4$ CUP OLIVE OIL, JUICE OF $1/2$ LEMON AND SALT. STAND 1 HOUR.

ADD CHOPPED FRESH HERBS — PARSLEY, THYME, CHIVES.

ZORBA THE MEATBALLS
GREEK MEATBALLS WITH MINT

ZORBA THE MEATBALLS IS A FINE MEAL.

A WAY OF MEETING NEW FRIENDS.

A TEST OF COURAGE.

ONE OF THE FEW RECIPES THAT CAN CHANGE YOUR LIFE.

BASIC PREPARATION:

I AM AT THIS VERY MOMENT STARING AT A WINE LABEL.

IT READS FOLLY HILL CHARDONNAY...A VERY SILLY WAY
TO SPELL CHARDONNET...AND THE YEAR OF WINE MAKING
IS 1990. IT IS FROM AUSTRALIA,

BUT THEN SO AM I. I HAVE DRUNK HALF A BOTTLE OF THIS
WINE AND INTEND TO FINISH THE BOTTLE AT ABOUT THE
SAME TIME AS I FINISH MAKING, NOT EATING, THE MEATBALLS.

IF ALL YOU WANT TO DO IS EAT SOME MEATBALLS AND
NOT CHANGE YOUR LIFE, IGNORE THE KNITTING NEEDLE,
THE PIECE OF STRING, THE BLACK BALACLAVA AND THE
GETAWAY CAR LISTED WITH THE OTHER INGREDIENTS.

IF YOU WANT TO CHANGE YOUR LIFE, PUT THE KNITTING
NEEDLE, THE PIECE OF STRING, THE BLACK BALACLAVA
AND THE FAST GETAWAY CAR TO ONE SIDE.

500G GROUND BEEF

4 SLICES WHITE BREAD

1 MEDIUM ONION, FINELY CHOPPED

1/2 CUP CHOPPED FRESH PARSLEY

1 EGG

1/2 CUP OLIVE OIL

2 TEASPOONS FRESH MINT

SALT

PEPPER

1 CLOVE CRUSHED GARLIC

1 CUP FLOUR

PINCH OF CINNAMON OR NUTMEG

PLACE MEAT IN A BOWL. DIP BREAD IN WATER AND SQUEEZE OUT EXCESS WATER. CRUMBLE BREAD AND ADD ALL OTHER INGREDIENTS TO THE MEAT. MIX WELL WITH YOUR HANDS.

PUT FLOUR ON A PLATE. SCOOP OUT TEASPOON-SIZE PIECES OF THE MIXTURE. ROLL INTO SMALL BALLS IN THE FLOUR, COATING WELL. BALLS CAN BE AS BIG AS YOU LIKE.

Heat oil in frypan and drop balls into hot oil, frying for 10-15 minutes until crisp and brown on all sides.

Serve with Egg & Lemon or Greek Tomato Sauce (page 56-57)

ZORBA THE MEATBALL CHANGE OF LIFE PROCEDURE

Put on the sound system the World War II song 'String of Pearls' by Glenn Miller. Very loud. Put holes in the meatballs with knitting needle.

Thread the string through the meatballs. tie the string.

Now you have a string of meatballs, just like a string of pearls.

Put them around your neck.

Put on the black balaclava.

In the fast getaway car drive to a public place, like a bar, or a football match or whatever.

TACTIC ONE:

Do nothing. Wait for people to ask obvious questions and then become manipulative depending on your wishes. Under no circumstances break any law except the general law of excessive weirdness.

TACTIC TWO:

APPROACH SELECTED PEOPLE WITH GREAT LINES LIKE
'HI, I'M CLINT...I'M HAVING A MEATBALL DINNER IN
A FEW DAYS FOR ELVIS PRESLEY AND BUDDY HOLLY.
WOULD YOU LIKE TO COME?'

* * *

I AM IN A WHITE ROOM. THE DOOR HAS WHITE PADDING.
I AM IN A WHITE JACKET THAT TIES AT THE BACK.
ZORBA THE MEATBALL HAS CHANGED MY LIFE.

NICE PEOPLE IN WHITE ARE PAYING MORE ATTENTION
TO ME THAN ANYONE EVER HAS BEFORE.

HERE COMES BARRY. HE GIVES ME MY AFTERNOON NEEDLE.

BARRY

POACHED OYSTERS WITH SPINACH IN CHAMPAGNE BUTTER

SERVES 6.

30 LEAVES OF ENGLISH SPINACH
1 SMALL ONION, FINELY CHOPPED
BUTTER
60ML DRY WHITE WINE
60ML FISH STOCK
100ML CREAM
250ML BUTTER, CUT IN CUBES
5 DOZEN OYSTERS
SALT AND PEPPER

REMOVE STALKS FROM SPINACH AND WASH WELL.

DROP INTO BOILING WATER FOR 15 SECONDS, REFRESH IN ICED WATER.

GENTLY FRY ONION IN BUTTER UNTIL TRANSLUCENT.

ADD WINE AND STOCK AND REDUCE BY HALF.

WHISK IN CREAM AND CUBED BUTTER, SIMMER GENTLY TO THICKEN SAUCE.

PUT ASIDE. WHEN READY TO SERVE, BRING SAUCE TO BOIL, TURN OFF HEAT AND ADD OYSTERS. STAND FOR 30 SECONDS. HEAT SPINACH IN A LITTLE BUTTER, SEASON, AND HEAP ONTO EACH PLATE.

SPOON OYSTER MIX ONTO SPINACH ON EACH PLATE.
(10 OYSTERS PER PERSON) AND POUR SAUCE OVER TOP.

LATE SUMMER SALAD

SALAD:	DRESSING:
ASPARAGUS	HAZELNUT OIL
BABY BEETROOT	TARRAGON VINEGAR
OYSTER MUSHROOMS	SALT AND PEPPER
MORELS	
GREEN BEANS	
VINEGAR	
SUGAR	
WALNUT OIL	
WHITE WINE	
MEAT GLAZE	

STEAM ASPARAGUS AND BEANS, REFRESH, CUT IN HALF.
BOIL BEETROOT WITH VINEGAR AND SUGAR, COOL, PEEL.
LIGHTLY FRY MUSHROOMS IN HAZELNUT OIL.
BRAISE MORELS IN WHITE WINE AND MEAT GLAZE.
COMBINE DRESSING INGREDIENTS, MIXING WELL. ARRANGE
SALAD DECORATIVELY ON PLATES AND POUR DRESSING OVER.

FRIED WHITEBAIT

1 CUP FLOUR
1 TEASPOON DILL TIPS
SALT AND PEPPER
OIL
500G WHITEBAIT
LEMON JUICE

PLACE FLOUR, DILL, SALT AND PEPPER IN A PLASTIC BAG.

TOSS WHITEBAIT IN MIX, THEN SHAKE THROUGH COLANDER TO REMOVE EXCESS FLOUR.

HEAT OIL UNTIL SMOKING, THEN FRY WHITEBAIT IN SMALL BATCHES UNTIL GOLDEN BROWN.

SERVE WITH LEMON JUICE AND SALAD.

SKEWERED FISH

500G WHITE FISH (BONELESS),
  CUT INTO CHUNKS
LEMON JUICE
THYME, ROSEMARY, SALT

DIP FISH INTO LEMON JUICE AND PUT 4-5 PIECES ON EACH SKEWER.

SPRINKLE WITH THYME AND ROSEMARY.

ADD SALT AND GRILL 5 MINUTES, TURNING ON ALL SIDES.

MARINATED BABY OCTOPUS

CRUSH 1 CLOVE GARLIC INTO OLIVE OIL, LEMON JUICE AND ROSEMARY OR OREGANO

GRILL UNTIL OCTOPUS CHANGES COLOUR.

DO NOT OVERCOOK.

CHICKEN LIVER AND CHAMPAGNE PATE

500G CHICKEN LIVERS

2 TABLESPOONS FLOUR

SALT AND PEPPER

2 CLOVES GARLIC

3 TABLESPOONS BACON FAT

125G MUSHROOMS, SLICED

$1/2$ CUP CHAMPAGNE

ROLL CHICKEN LIVERS IN FLOUR SEASONED WITH SALT AND PEPPER.

GENTLY FRY GARLIC IN BACON FAT FOR 2 MINUTES. INCREASE HEAT, ADD LIVERS AND COOK FOR A FEW MINUTES, TURNING. ADD MUSHROOMS. SEASON.

PLACE IN BLENDER, ADD CHAMPAGNE SLOWLY, BLENDING UNTIL MIXTURE IS SMOOTH. PUT IN CROCKERY POT AND CHILL WELL. SERVE WITH TOAST OR CRUSTY BREAD.

CONSTITUTION SQUARE KIDNEYS

LAMB KIDNEYS IN WINE SAUCE

1 KG LAMB KIDNEYS

1 TABLESPOON VINEGAR

2 TABLESPOONS FLOUR

2 TABLESPOONS BUTTER

2 TABLESPOONS OIL

1 CLOVE GARLIC, CRUSHED

SALT AND PEPPER

1 TEASPOON EACH OF OREGANO, MARJORAM, PARSLEY

1 BAY LEAF

1 CUP MUSHROOMS, SLICED

1 CUP RED WINE

RINSE KIDNEYS IN COLD WATER WITH A DASH OF VINEGAR. CUT OUT CORE, PAT DRY, SLICE AND ROLL IN FLOUR.

MELT BUTTER AND OIL IN A LARGE FRYING PAN.

FRY ON MEDIUM HEAT UNTIL LIGHTLY BROWNED ALL OVER.

ADD REMAINING INGREDIENTS.

COVER AND SIMMER 20 MINUTES, STIRRING SEVERAL TIMES.

GREEK VILLAGE BEAN SOUP

1 CUP DRIED BEANS (200G), WHITE, BROAD, LIMA, YELLOW OR GREEN SPLIT PEAS

2 LITRES COLD WATER

4 CELERY STALKS, FINELY DICED

2 ONIONS, FINELY DICED

1/4 TEASPOON DRIED OREGANO

1/4 TEASPOON DRIED THYME

1 TABLESPOON TOMATO PASTE

1 RED CAPSICUM, ROASTED AND PEELED

2 MEDIUM CARROTS, FINELY DICED

1 BAY LEAF

1/4 CUP OLIVE OIL

2 TEASPOONS SALT

PEPPER

SOAK BEANS OVERNIGHT, DRAIN, RINSE WELL.

HEAT OIL IN PAN OVER LOW HEAT. ADD VEGETABLES AND COOK OVER LOW HEAT.

BOIL BEANS IN THE WATER. REDUCE HEAT AND SIMMER FOR 1 HOUR.

ADD REMAINING INGREDIENTS AND SIMMER 1 1/2 HOURS UNTIL BEANS ARE TENDER.

SERVE WITH TOAST AND A CRUET OF OLIVE OIL AND VINEGAR.

EGG AND LEMON SAUCE

IS, IF THERE IS SUCH A THING, THE NATIONAL SAUCE
OF GREECE. IT IS POURED OVER SOUPS, MEATS,
VEGETABLES, POULTRY DISHES AND FISH.

3 EGGS
JUICE OF 3 LEMONS, STRAINED
1 CUP HOT BROTH

BEAT EGG WHITES UNTIL STIFF, ADD EGG YOLKS AND
CONTINUE TO BEAT EGGS UNTIL THICK AND FLUFFY —
AT LEAST 5 MINUTES IF USING AN ELECTRIC MIXER OR
10-15 MINUTES IF BY HAND.

ADD LEMON JUICE SLOWLY, BEATING ALL THE TIME.

MIX 1 CUP OF HOT BROTH INTO BEATEN EGGS,
STIRRING RAPIDLY WITH A SPOON TO PREVENT
CURDLING. POUR SAUCE OVER PREPREPARED DISH.

SERVE IMMEDIATELY. DO NOT REBOIL (IF YOU MUST
REHEAT, DO SO OVER A VERY LOW HEAT).

GREEK TOMATO SAUCE

2 TABLESPOONS OLIVE OIL

1 ONION, CHOPPED

1 CLOVE GARLIC, MINCED

1 400G CAN TOMATOES

SMALL CAN TOMATO PASTE

4 CUPS WATER

1/2 CUP WHITE WINE

1 TEASPOON SUGAR

2 TEASPOONS SALT

PEPPER

1/2 TEASPOON EACH OF FRESH BASIL, OREGANO, DRIED CINNAMON, PARSLEY, MINT

1 BAY LEAF

HEAT OIL, FRY ONION AND GARLIC FOR A FEW MINUTES.

ADD REMAINING INGREDIENTS.

BRING TO THE BOIL, REDUCE HEAT TO LOW AND SIMMER FOR 45 MINUTES, STIRRING OCCASIONALLY.

SERVE AS A SAUCE FOR PASTA, RICE, OR USE AS A BASE FOR CASSEROLES.

OIL AND LEMON DRESSING

¹/₂ CUP OLIVE OIL
JUICE OF 1 LEMON
¹/₄ TEASPOON OREGANO OR PARSLEY
¹/₄ TEASPOON SALT
WHITE PEPPER

WHISK INGREDIENTS TOGETHER.

USE OVER HOT OR COLD VEGETABLES, FRESH GREENS,
OLIVES AND FISH.

ALSO CAN BE USED AS A MARINADE OVER MEAT
AND FISH.

ARMADILLO-FREE RECIPE

WHITE SAUCE

2 TABLESPOONS CORNFLOUR
1/2 CUP COLD WATER
2 CUPS MILK
1 TABLESPOON BUTTER
1 1/2 TEASPOONS SALT
1 EGG, WELL BEATEN

DILUTE CORNFLOUR IN COLD WATER AND PUT TO ONE SIDE.

PLACE MILK, BUTTER AND SALT IN A POT AND BRING TO THE BOIL OVER A MEDIUM HEAT.

ADD THE DILUTED CORNFLOUR, STIRRING AS IT THICKENS.

REMOVE FROM HEAT, ADD SOME SAUCE TO BEATEN EGG, THEN ADD THE EGG TO THE SAUCE, MIXING IT IN WELL.

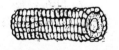

CORN

CORINTHIAN APPLE PITA

1/2 KG FILO PASTRY

FILLING:

8 COOKING APPLES, CORED, SEEDED AND CHOPPED

1/2 CUP SUGAR

1/2 TEASPOON EACH OF CINNAMON AND ALLSPICE

1 TABLESPOON CORNFLOUR

1/4 CUP ALMONDS

1/4 CUP CURRANTS

1/2 CUP CHOPPED WALNUTS

1/4 CUP CANNED CHERRIES, DRAINED

1/2 CUP MELTED BUTTER

TOPPING:

1 CUP OF ICING SUGAR

DEFROST FILO PASTRY TO ROOM TEMPERATURE – ABOUT 2-4 HOURS. MIX FILLING IN A BOWL.

LAY 5 SHEETS OF FILO FLAT, ONE ON TOP OF EACH OTHER, BRUSHING A LITTLE MELTED BUTTER BETWEEN EACH SHEET.

SPREAD 1 CUP OF THE FILLING ALONG ONE END.

ROLL FILO OVER THE FILLING, CREATING A LONG, FILLED TUBE.

FOLD SIDE EDGES OVER AS YOU ROLL, SO FILLING WON'T FALL OUT. ROLL UNTIL FINISHED.

PLACE IN A BUTTERED BAKING PAN.

BRUSH TOP GENEROUSLY WITH MELTED BUTTER.

BAKE IN MODERATE OVEN FOR 1 HOUR.

SIFT POWDERED SUGAR OVER THE TOP AND SIDES AS SOON AS IT IS TAKEN OUT OF THE OVEN.

WHEN COOL, CUT IN SLICES AND SERVE.

ATHENIAN CHEESECAKE

FILLING:

4 EGGS, SEPARATED
JUICE AND RIND OF 1 LEMON
1/2 CUP HONEY
1/2 KG CREAM OR COTTAGE CHEESE
1/3 CUP FLOUR
1 CUP SOUR CREAM

CRUST:

1 CUP SHORTBREAD BISCUIT CRUMBS
2 TABLESPOONS BUTTER
1/4 CUP GROUND ALMONDS

BEAT EGG WHITES UNTIL STIFF (WITH A PINCH OF SALT).

IN A BLENDER, BLEND EGG YOLKS, LEMON JUICE AND RIND, HONEY, CHEESE AND FLOUR FOR A FEW SECONDS.

FOLD BATTER INTO EGG WHITES. FOLD IN SOUR CREAM.

IN ANOTHER BOWL, MIX CRUMBS, NUTS AND BUTTER.

GREASE THE BOTTOMS AND SIDES OF A LARGE CAKE TIN.

SPREAD CRUMBS OVER BOTTOM AND UP SIDES.

POUR IN MIXTURE.

BAKE IN MODERATE OVEN FOR 45 MINUTES.

CHILL FOR AT LEAST 6 HOURS BEFORE CUTTING.

SESAME HONEY STICKS PASTELLE

1 CUP SESAME SEEDS
1 CUP HONEY

SPREAD SESAME SEEDS IN A SMALL BAKING DISH AND TOAST IN A MODERATE (PREHEATED) OVEN FOR 5 MINUTES.

BOIL HONEY.

ADD THE SESAME SEEDS AND CONTINUE COOKING ON A MEDIUM HEAT UNTIL LIGHTLY CRACKING. WATCH CAREFULLY AS IT BURNS EASILY!

POUR INTO BUTTERED PAN AND FLATTEN UNTIL $1\frac{1}{2}$ CM THICK. CUT INTO 5 CM PIECES WHILE HOT. COOL. CAN BE STORED IN A PLASTIC BAG.

HALVAH FUDGE

2 CUPS BROWN SUGAR
$2/3$ CUP MILK
$2/3$ CUP TAHINI
1 TEASPOON VANILLA

COOK SUGAR AND MILK OVER MEDIUM HEAT TO JUST UNDER THE SOFT BALL STAGE. (THIS IS WHERE YOU CAN TEST THE MIXTURE BY FORMING A BALL WHEN YOU DROP A SMALL AMOUNT ONTO A COLD SURFACE.)

REMOVE FROM STOVE AND ADD TAHINI AND VANILLA, BUT DON'T MIX IN STRAIGHTAWAY – COOL FOR ABOUT 2 MINUTES.

BEAT WITH WOODEN SPOON FOR SEVERAL SECONDS AND POUR QUICKLY INTO A BUTTERED PAN.

Greek Islands
Identification Chart

Ten unexpected Greek islands from the south

HYDRA

ANDROS

MYKONOS

SANTORINI

PAROS

NAXOS

CHIOS

LIMNOS

LESBOS

SAMOS